The Story of Spring
The First Flower

Rosie McCormick

HODDER
Wayland

an imprint of Hodder Children's Books

Text copyright © Rosie McCormick 2005

Editor: Kirsty Hamilton
Design: Proof Books

Published in Great Britain in 2005
by Hodder Wayland, an imprint of
Hodder Children's Books

The publishers would like to thank the following for allowing us to reproduce their pictures in this book: Corbis: Douglas Peebles title page; Owen Franken 3; Steve Austin, Paphilio 4; Donna Disario 5; Lucido Studio, Inc 6; Geray Sweeney 7; Roger Wilmshurst, Frank Lane Picture Agency 8; Mark Gibson 9; John Tinning, Frank Lane Picture Agency 10; Chase Swift 11; Sylvain Saustier 12; Richard Cummins 13; Lester Lefkowitz 14; Jim Foster 15; Seman Design Grp 16; Roy Morsch 17; Kevin R. Morris 19; Jack Fields 20; Robert Essel NYC 21; Eric and David Hosking 22; William Manning 23 / Getty Images: Jim Cummins, Taxi 18.

British Library Cataloguing in Publication Data
McCormick, Rosie
The first flower : the story of spring. – (The story of the seasons)
1.Spring – Juvenile literature
I.Title
508.2

ISBN 0 7502 46243

Printed in China

Hodder Children's Books
A division of Hodder Headline Limited
338 Euston Road, London NW1 3BH

Contents

The earth's magic

The late winter landscape is quiet and still. But slowly, as the early spring sunshine grows brighter and stronger, the glistening winter frosts make way for early-morning dew. And all around astonishing things begin to happen.

Tiny new leaves that have been curled up inside plant and tree buds, burst out. In the warm sunshine they grow bigger and greener. Birds that had flown away to warmer places return, and sleeping creatures begin to wake – all because spring has arrived.

5

The first flower

As the frozen land begins to thaw, the first flowers emerge. Snowdrops and crocuses provide a delicate splash of colour across the grey, frozen landscape. Then, gradually, as the spring sunshine continues to warm the earth, daffodils as yellow as the sun and ruby-red tulips burst into life. The fragrant smell of springtime is carried through the air.

6

The cold days of winter are behind us at last, and the promise of springtime is here.

The long journey home

As buds, blossoms and flowers burst into life, the silent woodlands, fields and lake shores begin to echo with familiar sounds. "Choooowww, chooooowwww," "Caawwww, Caaawww". Birds, such as swifts, swallows, geese and ducks fly hundreds, even thousands of miles to their spring homes. Once there they will gather twigs and other materials to build nests and have their young.

And for animals that have slept through the winter months in hidden nests or stayed warm in deeply dug tunnels, it's time to wake up and venture outside once again.

Food for all

For the animals that have struggled to survive during the dark, cold, lifeless days of winter, the first signs of spring mean food, light, warmth and a chance to find a mate. Although animals like badgers and foxes have thick winter coats to keep them warm during the coldest, harshest months, the search for food is never easy. Many animals are lucky to have survived.

New life

Gradually fields and meadows burst into life.
They grow green and lush and will soon be used
for grazing. And with spring come the sights and
sounds of new life. It is the time for lambs, calves,
foals, chicks and young of all kind to be born.
Throughout the spring and summer, nature will
provide all the things these young animals need.
They will grow bigger and stronger. Strong
enough to cope with winter, when it comes again.

13 🌸

The rich earth

As winter turns into spring, farmers work hard to prepare the land for planting. The soil must be turned and fed, ready for spring crops. The crops will flourish with the help of the spring rains and the summer sunshine.

This is an essential part of the natural cycle. For the crops
planted in spring, and harvested in late summer and early autumn,
provide food for people and animals during the winter months when
little can grow in the frozen earth.

15

Winds blow

Although the spring sunlight now warms and revives the land, and the days are much brighter, the skies can still be ominous. Strong, blustery winds can blow fierce and cold. And dark, thunderous rain clouds can sweep across the sky. Winds can blow umbrellas inside out, and remind us that winter has only just retreated.

But spring winds are eagerly awaited by some. They can blow strong enough for colourful kites to take to the skies and do battle with the winds.

16

Rain and shine

With winter almost a memory, gardens and parks become full of the sights and sounds of people enjoying the arrival of spring. But don't forget that nature likes to surprise us. During springtime there are often unexpected showers and spectacular rainbows that colour the sky after the rainfall.

18

Beautiful blossom

For thousands of years the longed for arrival of spring has been celebrated in a variety of ways. In Japan, the 'land of flowers', blossom festivals, or *O-hanami,* are held in honour of the sweetly scented spring cherry blossom. In Japan, the cherry blossom symbolises the fertility of the earth and the arrival of the new season. People sing and dance and celebrate together, for it is indeed a magical time.

The making of spring and summer

AN ANCIENT GREEK MYTH

Long ago, the god of the heavens Zeus, and the goddess of nature Demeter, had a daughter called Persephone. She was much loved. But the fearful Hades, god of the underworld, stole her away to the dark underworld. No one could find Persephone.

Because of her grief Demeter forgot about nature's harvest. And so a famine struck the land. Until one day, the god Apollo discovered the captured Persephone.

Zeus sent a messenger to the underworld to bring her back. But her captor Hades had played a terrible trick. This trickery meant that she was bound to the underworld for six months each year. And so it is that Demeter only brings life and warmth to the land when her daughter is free of her dark prison.

Glossary

Blossom – spring flowers on hedges and trees

Bud – a shoot from which a flower or leaf grows

Burrow – a hole or tunnel dug by an animal

Crops – plants grown by people for food

Den – the home of a wild animal

Dew – drops of water that gather on plants at night

Frost – water that freezes on plants at night

Harvest – when ripe crops are gathered

Meadow – land that is watered by a river

Rainbow – colours that appear in the sky when it is sunny and rainy

Survive – to stay alive

Index